DO IT NOW!

W9-CCD-575

ANDY BRUCE
& KEN LANGDON

LONDON, NEW YORK, SYDNEY, DELHI, PARIS
MUNICH, & JOHANNESBURG

Senior Editor Nina Hathaway
Senior Designer Jamie Hanson
DTP Designer Julian Dams
Production Controllers Alistair Rogerson,
Michelle Thomas

US Editors Gary Werner, and
Margaret Parrish

Managing Editor Adèle Hayward
Senior Managing Editor Stephanie Jackson
Senior Managing Art Editor Nigel Duffield

Produced for DK by

studio **cactus** Ⓒ

13 SOUTHGATE STREET WINCHESTER HAMPSHIRE SO23 9DZ

Editor Kate Hayward
Designer Laura Watson

First American Edition 2001

01 02 03 04 05 10 9 8 7 6 5 4 3 2 1

Published in the United States by
DK Publishing, Inc.
95 Madison Avenue
New York, New York 10016

Copyright © 2001 Dorling Kindersley Limited
Text copyright © 2001 Ken Langdon and Andy Bruce

All rights reserved under International and Pan-
American Copyright Conventions. No part of this
publication may be reproduced, stored in a retrieval
system, or transmitted in any form or by any means,
electronic, mechanical, photocopying, recording, or
otherwise, without the prior written permission of the
copyright owner. Published in Great Britain by Dorling
Kindersley Limited.

A Cataloging in Publication record is available from the
Library of Congress

ISBN 0-7894-8006-9

Reproduced by Colourscan, Singapore
Printed and bound in Hong Kong by Wing King Tong

See our complete catalog at
www.dk.com

CONTENTS

4 INTRODUCTION

PREPARING TO DO IT NOW

6 DEFINING THE TERM

8 KNOWING YOUR OBJECTIVES

10 CHOOSING TO ACT

12 ACTING EFFECTIVELY

14 STARTING TO ACT NOW

18 DECIDING NOT TO ACT

TAKING ACTION NOW

20 CREATING A TO-DO LIST

24 USING TIME WISELY

26 AVOIDING PROCRASTINATION

28 MAKING
THINGS HAPPEN

30 INVOLVING
OTHERS

DECIDING
LOGICALLY

32 VALUING
THINKING

36 UNDERSTANDING
CAUSES

38 USING A
PROCESS

42 TAKING
SHORTCUTS

44 TURNING A DECISION
INTO ACTION

GETTING
ORGANIZED

46 GATHERING
FACTS

48 STRUCTURING YOUR
INFORMATION

52 UNDERSTANDING
TECHNOLOGY OPTIONS

54 HARNESSING
TECHNOLOGIES

56 HELPING OTHERS
TO DO IT NOW

LEARNING
FROM EXPERIENCE

58 FOCUSING ON
IMPROVING

60 CAPTURING BEST
PRACTICES

62 SHARING
INSIGHTS

64 LEADING A
BALANCED LIFE

66 ASSESSING YOUR SKILLS
AS A DO-IT-NOW PERSON

70 INDEX

72 ACKNOWLEDGMENTS

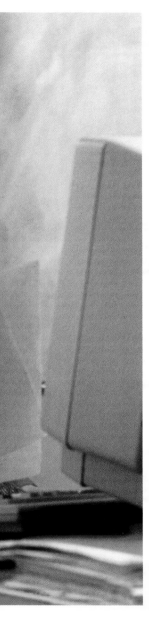

INTRODUCTION

*A*chieving objectives on schedule and within budget is crucial to the success of any organization. *Do It Now!* considers the main causes of delay and inefficiency in a business environment, and offers practical ways to help you and your team identify objectives, prioritize actions, organize time efficiently, tackle issues as they arise, and use experience as an element of the decision-making process. Throughout the book, 101 tips offer practical advice to help you improve working routines, while a self-assessment questionnaire allows you to evaluate your performance and keep track of your progress. Adopting a do-it-now approach will enable you to maximize the performance of your organization while allowing you to optimize your leisure time, making you more efficient in all aspects of your life.

PREPARING TO DO IT NOW

People who operate on a do-it-now basis focus on the important activities they need to complete in order to meet their objectives. Make a start on working more effectively.

DEFINING THE TERM

A do-it-now person can be relied on to get work done in time. Such people do not put anything off until later, whether the issue involves taking immediate action, thinking matters through, or gathering the facts necessary to make a decision.

 Understand that proactive people do the right things on time.

▲ **CREATING TEAM SPIRIT**
Do-it-now people create and maintain excellent relationships with their team, colleagues, and business partners.

WHY DO IT NOW?

Some business people consistently meet their performance targets by dealing with the right issues in the right order. They are in control of both their personal and business lives, and their colleagues rely on them. Do-it-now people have to cope with stress in their business lives like everyone else, but their well-organized approach and ability to cope with the issues of the day in a timely fashion allow them to keep stress to a minimum. Finally, when do-it-now people go home, they leave work behind them entirely, knowing that their tasks are under control.

2 Make sure that you keep everyone informed about when a task will be completed.

▼ **WORKING PROACTIVELY**
A proactive person reviews a task on receipt, schedules it, and then informs the relevant parties of a completion date.

ANALYZING OTHERS

Think about the people you work with. Divide them into do-it-now people and the put-it-off gang. Think about what distinguishes one group from the other. Do-it-now people will never need reminding that they have a task to complete, and they will tell you when to expect the task to be done. Conversely, you never know where you are with people who put things off. If, for example, they are having difficulty with a task, they fail to inform you and you find out that something has gone wrong only when the completion date has passed. Decide which category of person your colleagues would put you into.

Review	→	**Schedule**	→	**Inform**

RESOLVING TO CHANGE

Decide now to become a do-it-now person. This may require you to make significant changes to the way you work. Getting organized may involve, for example, changing your filing systems, using a new system for making decisions, or implementing a new way of prioritizing actions. Remember, however, that it is also a matter of getting your attitude right when taking control of your work.

Communicates effectively

Takes initiative

Responds efficiently

Improves processes

Prioritizes actions

▲ **AIMING TO DO IT NOW**
The qualities that a do-it-now person possesses lead to a reputation for reliability and for being able to complete actions successfully, on time, and with the minimum of stress.

3 Be a proactive person who initiates actions, rather than a reactive one who waits to be prompted.

KNOWING YOUR OBJECTIVES

A do-it-now person is quite clear about what his or her goals are. Decide what your objectives are and begin to separate what you must do to achieve these objectives from any other matters that call on your time. Be ruthless in avoiding unnecessary work.

4 Prepare specific objectives and agree on them with your manager.

5 Sort the important tasks from any unnecessary ones.

6 Make sure your job description is up to date and still relevant.

FOCUSING ON YOUR AIMS

Other tasks often distract you from your real responsibilities. Distinguish between the actions and information that directly contribute to your business success and the other issues that infringe on your workload. Be quite clear about your objectives and remind yourself of what you are aiming for. Refer to your job description, if you have one, or ask your team leader for their view of your job and use this as a basis for your job description so that you can set your objectives.

▼ ANALYZING YOUR ROLE

In this example, an employee is discussing his role with his manager so that he can begin to set his short- and long-term objectives and start to form definite goals to work toward.

Employee listens to manager's perspective before determining his objectives

Manager outlines her view of employee's role

Notes are useful for future reference

SETTING YOUR OBJECTIVES

Work out your objectives by listing the key areas of your job in order of importance. Limit the number of objective areas to six and choose active words to describe your objectives. Add the percentage of time you need to put into each area. Make sure that you can measure your achievements in each area and consider the best ways to monitor your performance, for example, through customer feedback or regular reviews.

List objectives

Set amount of time

Objective	Measure	Percentage of time
To maintain customer satisfaction.	Reduction in complaints received from 10% of sales to 5%.	20%
To answer telephones promptly.	90% of calls to be answered within three rings.	30%
To train new team member.	New team member can work on their own.	50% of time for first two months, then review.

Agree on performance measures

▲ DOCUMENTING OBJECTIVES

The more specific and clear you make your objectives, the more focused your work will be. Make sure you include performance measures that you and your team leader have agreed to.

7 Remember, once you have identified your objectives, you can focus your mind on them.

BEING CRITICAL

List all the things that you do currently and put them into the order in which they impact your performance. The clearer your vision of what you are trying to achieve, the easier it will be to get things into the right order. Now create a second list, using your calendar or your activity reporting system, of your work activities in order of the time you spend on each one. Compare the two lists. If they are both in the same order, you are focusing on what is important for achieving your objectives.

Compares lists against calendar

COMPARING LISTS ▶

If you find that the list of your objective priority ratings is very different from your daily schedule, you are going to have to change your priorities and methods.

CHOOSING TO ACT

Sometimes it is best to deal with an issue immediately, and other times it is better to leave it for a more appropriate time. Choose whether to act immediately, deal with it later, or decide to delay action while you gather more information.

8 Recognize the routine triggers you should react to automatically.

STIMULATING ACTION

Think about what stimulates you to act. It may be a customer, your manager, or a stimulus such as an order form. Some triggers are regularly going to be more important to the achievement of your objectives than others. Work out which these are. Make sure these triggers happen early enough for you to be able to deal with them in time. If you are ordering materials from a supplier, for example, ensure the system gives you enough time to allow for delivery.

▼ **RECEIVING TRIGGERS**
In this example, an administrator found that a trigger for action came too late for her to be able to achieve her objectives efficiently, and this affected her colleagues.

CASE STUDY

Sally took on the responsibility of moving people's belongings from one workplace to another when they moved to a new office or department. To do this she had to organize the provision of crates for the movers before the actual move was due. She then had to get movers to handle the move. The movers were contractors, and it cost Sally's organization money if their work was postponed. Although she organized the delivery of the boxes as soon as she had notice of a move, many people complained that they did not have enough time to pack their things. Sally talked it over with her colleague in Human Resources who changed their system to make sure that Sally was informed earlier of an impending move. This gave Sally the opportunity to get the boxes to the right place and give the movers at least a week to pack.

QUESTIONS TO ASK YOURSELF

Q Do I know which triggers prompt me to take action?

Q Do I recognize these triggers early enough to be able to take effective action?

Q How can I get an earlier trigger in areas that require an urgent response?

ACTING IMMEDIATELY

On receiving a trigger, it may be appropriate to act immediately. You may have encountered the situation before or there may be a set procedure in place. In these circumstances, you should act now rather than putting off the action. Act now when you have all the information you need to respond to the trigger, and you do not need any thinking time to decide what needs to be done.

MAKING DECISIONS

Some triggers offer you options of what action to take, and in this situation, the correct response to the stimulus is to make a decision. Suppose a team member reports a problem with a computer terminal. If you know that they are inexperienced with the terminal, you may choose to go and see if you can make it work. If you know the team member to be expert in using the terminal, you may choose to call for technical help immediately.

9   Act now if you already know what needs to be done.

10   Gather relevant data before you make a decision.

GETTING INFORMATION

With some stimuli, it may be impossible to act immediately. In fact, an immediate response can cause problems if you make the wrong decision. It may also be impossible to act if you do not have all the information. Recognize when this is the case. Initiate actions to gather the facts you need to make a decision. Often, the best response is to gather as much information as you can.

▼ RESPONDING TO TRIGGERS
It is not always right to act immediately. There may be more than one possible response, or you may need to spend time gathering more information in order to take appropriate action.

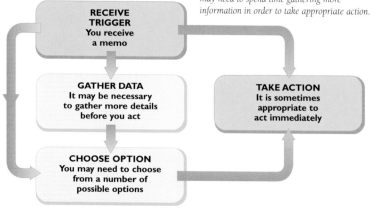

RECEIVE TRIGGER
You receive a memo

GATHER DATA
It may be necessary to gather more details before you act

TAKE ACTION
It is sometimes appropriate to act immediately

CHOOSE OPTION
You may need to choose from a number of possible options

ACTING EFFECTIVELY

It is not enough to make a decision on whether to act immediately based solely on triggers. Take the time to think about acting in a way that gets the most effective results in the future, and look continuously for ways to improve procedures.

 11 Critique your working processes and seek ways to improve them.

THINGS TO DO

1. Look at your working procedures.
2. Check whether all the tasks you carry out are necessary.
3. Decide which actions are repetitive and unnecessary.
4. Think about how you could start to work differently.

ANALYZING PROCESSES

Whenever something prompts you to action, take time to analyze it. If it is routine, check that the routine is still the best way to get things done. Think about it as though you were your team leader. Would you change the process involved in dealing with the issue? Is there a better way of acting? If the stimulus is not routine, decide whether an initiative from you would have improved the situation. Even when you are acting on an instruction, make sure that it contributes to your objectives. Discuss an issue if you consider it to be a distraction from your main task.

IMPROVING PROCESSES

Many actions are part of normal business processes. Such processes evolve over time and, sometimes, this evolution introduces actions or paperwork that are not directly necessary to any critical part of the process. Think about the processes that you are involved in. What parts of them are critical? What parts could you cut out with no adverse effects? Reexamine all your routines in this way. Consider new processes that could help you achieve the same goal in less time. Get rid of any unnecessary routines.

Notes possible changes to routines

Analyzes procedures

▲ ANALYZING EFFECTIVENESS

Take the time to think through your routines and methods of working. Continuously seek ways to improve your effectiveness and efficiency.

IMPROVING A ROUTINE PROCEDURE TO BOOST PERFORMANCE

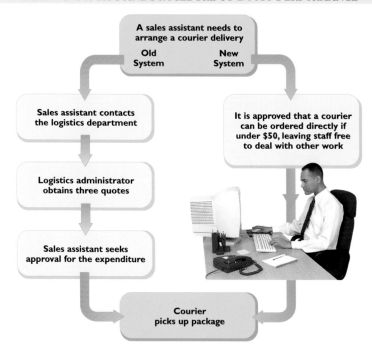

A sales assistant needs to arrange a courier delivery

| Old System | New System |

Sales assistant contacts the logistics department

It is approved that a courier can be ordered directly if under $50, leaving staff free to deal with other work

Logistics administrator obtains three quotes

Sales assistant seeks approval for the expenditure

Courier picks up package

BECOMING PROACTIVE

How much of your time is taken up responding to stimuli, and how much is spent on activities that you have planned? Work toward a point where most of your actions are planned. If you spend a lot of time "fire fighting," consider the cause of the delay. Always take action at the right time irrespective of whether or not the task is difficult. Resolve to deal with the causes of problems even if you then delay your reaction to an issue others consider to be urgent. This means that, as well as reacting to events, you are starting the process of making a crisis less likely in the future.

12 Look at whether or not you put off difficult tasks.

13 Remember, if you put things off, a problem can turn into a crisis.

STARTING TO ACT NOW

T*he do-it-now culture is a way of life. Think about other people's reactions to the way you work and start adopting proactive habits. Learn to deal with information in the most effective way and work on your reputation for reliability.*

14 Note down ideas that might lead you to better ways of doing things.

RECORDING IDEAS

A magazine article or a conversation with one of your friends can spark ideas about how you go about your work. Carry a notebook or a personal organizer to capture these ideas. These insights may help you to achieve your objectives or improve the way that you work. Remember, once a great idea is recorded it can never die.

Colleague discusses how he dealt with a difficult customer

Team member keeps notepad on hand to write down ideas

COLLECTING INSIGHTS ▶
Listen to your friends and colleagues talking about their work. You may find that they have habits that you could adopt yourself. Note any good ideas for your own reference.

QUESTIONS TO ASK YOURSELF

Q Do I let people know when I have heard from them?

Q Do I tell people how and by when I will react?

Q Do I take charge of meeting other people's expectations?

Q Do I let people know when they have sent me material that is not relevant to me?

KEEPING IN TOUCH

M ost people have had the experience of sending finished work to a person and hearing nothing in reply. If you receive no reaction, you wonder first of all whether the work was received, and then you start to worry that the recipient does not like your work. Remember that other people feel the same way when they correspond with you. Start to respond immediately to every communication you receive. If you do not need the material you have been sent, tell the sender in a response.

RESPONDING TO A COMMUNICATION

ACTIONS REQUIRED	APPROPRIATE RESPONSE
RESPOND AND ACT NOW	Act immediately if you know what the correct action is, and have all the necessary information on hand.
RESPOND AND SCHEDULE	If immediate action is impossible, schedule when you will carry out the action and inform the appropriate people.
RESPOND AND REFER	If you are not the appropriate recipient, refer the communication on and advise the sender.
RESPOND AND FILE	If the information received is useful but requires no action, advise the sender and file for future reference.
RESPOND AND DISCARD	If the communication is irrelevant, inform the sender. Try to prevent irrelevant material from reaching you in future.

WORKING WITH OTHERS

Just as you want other people to understand what they should expect from you, you need to know what you should expect from other people. Make sure you understand the responsibilities of the people on your team. When you delegate an action, make sure you are referring it to the appropriate person and that he or she will accept responsibility for it. Realize that it is not enough to ask someone to do something and use this as an excuse if nothing happens.

15 Set people's expectations at an achievable level.

Supplies schedule to team member via email

Telephones team member to emphasize the deadline

FOLLOWING UP ▶
If you delegate work, make it clear what you expect others to do. Follow up actions to make sure that they are successfully completed.

DEALING WITH DATA

Everyone is beset by incoming data. Look around at the desks in your place of work. Notice the sense of order on the desktops of proactive colleagues. When you receive new data, aim to deal with it immediately by making a decision to act, filing it in an accessible place for future use, or by discarding any irrelevant material. If you need to keep an in-tray, make sure that it does not become a permanent resting place for old, unfiled paperwork.

16 Keep filing up to date and easily accessible.

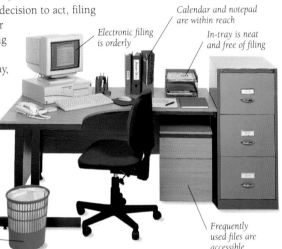

Calendar and notepad are within reach

Electronic filing is orderly

In-tray is neat and free of filing

BEING ORDERLY ▶
Keep your working area and filing systems orderly so that you can access and make good use of information easily.

Unnecessary data is discarded

Frequently used files are accessible

PRESENTING EMAILS

It is best to keep email correspondence short and to the point. Make sure that your messages are clear and leave no room for misinterpretation. If a matter requires a lot of explanation, it may be better to communicate it by telephone or face-to-face. Although you can flag emails as "urgent," use this device sparingly. Remember to keep formatting, such as bullet points or hyphenation, to a minimum, as this can be altered in transmission to other people's systems.

IMPROVING PRESENTATION

Consider the data that you receive from other parts of your organization. Ask yourself in every case whether the current method of presentation makes the data useful to you, or do you have to do some work to find out what you need? This is often the case. Solve this problem by talking to the sender of the data. If it is easy for them to change the presentation to suit your needs, it will save you time. Look at data you usually ignore and assess whether it could be presented in a way you might find useful.

AVOIDING PERFECTIONISM

Try to avoid analysis paralysis. Many decisions are based on less than perfect information. Avoid waiting for more information if it means that you will decide or take action too late. Time is money and waiting for data is counterproductive if the delay costs more than taking action earlier. If you put something off, you have to go through material again in order to remember the details. If you take action immediately on a matter that, with the benefit of hindsight, was not strictly necessary, the waste of energy is compensated for by the time you saved in acting quickly.

17 Recognize that the perfect answer can arrive too late.

18 Remember that acting immediately takes less time than putting actions off.

POINTS TO REMEMBER

● It is only useful to gather more information if you use it to increase your understanding.

● You should avoid collecting and filing information if it is not actually of use to you personally.

● A large percentage of filed papers are never referred to because they were not required in the first place.

● As your job changes, so does your need for information.

DISTINGUISHING BETWEEN INFORMATION AND DATA

Whenever data arrives at your workspace, always assess what is information and what is simply data. Data is a series of available facts or opinions. Information is made up of facts that will help you in your operational life or offer insights into your strategic thinking. For data to be information, it must have value to you. Make this clear in your mind so that you begin to look for data to increase your effectiveness, rather than merely close gaps. Think about this as you strive to reduce clutter.

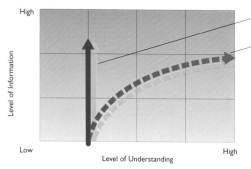

Data is collected without aiding understanding

Information is used to develop new insights

◀ USING DATA

When you start a project, it is tempting to gather a lot of data. Instead, focus on information that you actually require so that you can start working on the project and learn how to make improvements. Here, the red-dotted line shows that data is being used to increase understanding.

DECIDING NOT TO ACT

The proactive choice can be deciding not to do something. If an action that you are about to undertake is not relevant to your objectives, consider not doing it. Make and explain your choice rather than ignoring what others see as a commitment.

19 Realize that it is sometimes more effective to decide not to take action.

QUESTIONS TO ASK YOURSELF

Q Have I checked that there is a real problem that needs to be acted on?

Q What would be the effect if I did nothing about this?

Q Who should I ask so that I can ascertain whether action is really necessary?

Q Am I the right person to act on this?

Q If I do nothing and it becomes important, will I be able to do it later?

ASKING "SO WHAT?"

When action is called for, make sure you respond immediately. Sometimes that response will be to ask yourself, "So what?" Suppose, for example, a supplier fails to deliver the computer equipment that you were due to install in another department. Rather than sourcing the equipment immediately from somewhere else, ask yourself what the delay actually means. Check that there are no other actions concerned with the project that mean that the late delivery will delay the completion of the installation. You may decide you do need to take action, but check first.

CASE STUDY

In a training course on decision making, a sales assistant, Alice, raised the point: "While I understand the elements of the decision-making process you are giving us, I do not see where I would be able to use them in my work." Andrew, the trainer, tried to ask questions and make suggestions to solve this problem. After 20 unsuccessful minutes the group moved on from this point.

During the coffee break Andrew explained what had happened to his team leader. The leader suggested that rather than immediately answering such a question, Andrew should try "doing nothing." On the next occasion that a person expressed a similar doubt, Andrew deliberately did nothing and, within a few seconds, other course delegates explained how they used the tool with their own real examples.

◀ **GETTING THE RIGHT RESPONSE**

In this example, a trainer conducting a training course realized that it is sometimes better not to try to solve a problem immediately, but to leave it for a more appropriate moment. He saw that, in some instances, problems can resolve themselves.

DOING NOTHING

There are occasions when, after asking the "So what?" question, the right response to a stimulus may be to do nothing. If you suspect that something could harm your performance, but you believe the risk that it will happen to be small, then taking action to counter the threat may be a poor use of your time. Realize that some problems simply go away. This may be, for example, because someone else tackles them. Some problems will be easy to recover from even if they persist.

DECIDING WHETHER TO DO NOTHING ▼
Analyze a problem when it arises and check whether it could cause damage to the achievement of your objectives. If it will not have an adverse effect, decide to do nothing.

20 Check that you are taking action because you actually need to.

21 Remember, if you do decide to do nothing, tell the relevant people.

| Analyze | ➤ | Check | ➤ | Do Nothing |

▲ COMMUNICATING A DECISION
Discuss a decision not to act with your customer. Your customer may agree with you, suggest a possible solution, or point out the reasons why it is important that you do take action.

INFORMING PEOPLE

The key to a decision not to act is to ensure that you inform the people involved. Deciding not to act is then a proactive choice. If you do not inform others of your decision, they may expect action and feel let down when nothing happens. A salesman, for example, who thinks that a customer is unlikely to prefer his solution to his competitor's, may decide not to take part in a tender. He must tell his client. The reaction of colleagues or clients can be interesting. They may well agree with the decision.

TAKING ACTION NOW

Action now is often more effective than action later. Decide what needs to be done, make sure that your decision is based on a good understanding of the facts, then do it now.

CREATING A TO-DO LIST

The starting point for getting organized is your action list, or to-do list. This document controls what you do and when you do it. Draw up a to-do list with all the entries relevant to your operational responsibilities, and prioritize your time.

> **22** Be ruthless in taking irrelevant actions off your to-do list.

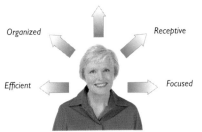

Forward-thinking

Organized

Receptive

Efficient

Focused

▲ **THINKING PROACTIVELY**
Do-it-now people are efficient not only because they focus on objectives, but also because they recognize the need to review and change their working processes.

MAKING YOUR LIST

Start by making a to-do list that is up to date. Make sure that it is comprehensive and incorporates all the operational matters that need to be done, while also including what you need to do to plan ahead. Your list will then include actions that are important for the present as well as the long term. Go through the list looking for actions that make no contribution toward achieving your objectives. Assess these actions and whether they must remain on your list.

ALLOCATING STATUS

Sort the list according to the status of the activity. If the action is straightforward, and you have all the information you require to carry it out, allocate it status "green." If you are unsure how to do the action, or you need further information, allocate that action "amber." "Red" status actions are those that you know are going to give you a problem. For example, if you know that an activity involves expenditure that will cause you to exceed your budget, give it status "red." Discard any unnecessary actions.

23 See if there are any tasks that you could delegate.

24 Make sure you are not doing other people's work.

	Topic	Actions	Status	Date
Use categories to clarify areas of action	Reserve facilities	1. Get three quotes	Green	June 19th
		2. Check with speakers what visual aids they need	Green	
		3. Place order with full requirement described	Green	
List all tasks involved	Brief Participants	1. Agree joining instructions with conference leader	Green	June 25th
		2. Issue joining instructions	Green	
	Secure budget	1. Calculate travel and subsistence budget	Amber	June 30th
		2. Prepare total budget	Green	
		3. Present and agree on with Finance Director	Red	

◀ **COMPILING A TO-DO LIST**
In this example of a to-do list, the tasks involved in planning a conference are subdivided into their relevant categories.

Schedule date that actions should be completed by

Allocate status for each action on list

25 Review your to-do list frequently and discuss it with your team on a regular basis.

DISCUSSING THE LIST

Your to-do list now reflects what you think needs to be done and what problems you are going to have to overcome. Now talk through your list with the members of your team so that you get another perspective on your main aims. They may help you to see that some actions are unnecessary. The status of an action may be reduced by a change in your objectives – for example, by the allocation of extra funds to your budget from a source that is known to be underspent.

USING ABC ANALYSIS

Assess the priority of each action. Rate actions that are crucial to the achievement of your performance objectives as category "A," and include difficult actions that are still critical. Label actions that will have a lesser impact on your performance, or ones that are not yet urgent, as category "B." Each day, prioritize the A-rated actions first and, when you can make no more progress with them, go on to the B-rated activities. Allocate "C" to the rest of the to-do list.

ASSESSING YOUR PRIORITIES

Decide which actions are critical to your objectives

Consider which actions have a lesser impact or are not urgent

Allocate a priority rating to each item on your list

Concentrate your actions each day on your top priorities

DOS AND DON'TS

✔ Do be analytical and honest with your priority ratings.

✔ Do test all C-rated actions to make sure they are relevant.

✔ Do act on difficult actions first rather than delaying them.

✘ Don't give priority to actions just because you enjoy them.

✘ Don't be afraid to discard actions on your list.

✘ Don't concentrate on one task to the detriment of others.

26 Use your priority ratings to schedule your work.

Each action on to-do list is allocated priority rating A, B, or C

Topic	Actions	Status	Priority	Date
Book facilities	1. Get three quotes	Green	A	June 19th
	2. Check with speakers what visual aids they need	Green	B	
	3. Place order with full requirement described	Green	B	
Brief Participants	1. Agree joining instructions with conference leader	Green	C	June 25th
	2. Issue joining instructions	Green	C	
Secure budget	1. Calculate travel and subsistence budget	Amber	B	June 30th
	2. Prepare total budget	Green	B	
	3. Present and agree on with Finance Director	Red	B	

◀ SCHEDULING YOUR ACTIONS
Concentrate on category A actions first, followed by category B actions. Work on category C actions when you can make no further progress with the A and B categories, or when the urgency of a C-rated action increases and you have to rerate it.

Date is set for when actions need to be completed by

27 Ensure your team understands the difference between what is important and what is urgent.

TAKING CONTROL

Some actions will be considered urgent by you or your colleagues. Make sure that they are also important before you agree to do them urgently. An urgent action is one that needs to be done now, but an important action is one that is vital to achieving your objectives. Explain to your manager if a task he or she thinks is urgent is actually not important to you. Your manager may delegate the action to someone else, or change your objectives to reflect a new business requirement.

KEEPING CONTROL

In the long term, take such good control of your business life that you reduce the number of urgent actions on your list, even though you are unlikely to remove them completely. If you find yourself regularly dealing with things that have high urgency and high impact, then you are still in fire-fighting mode. The ideal is to look ahead and foresee problems and opportunities before they become urgent. When you find that much of your time is spent on actions that are high impact but low urgency, you have things under control.

28 Give yourself the time to take opportunities.

29 Predict and prevent problems before they occur.

BEING SELFISH WITH YOUR TIME

Many people may make demands on your time. It is important that you, not they, make the decisions about what is high priority and what is low priority. If someone is putting pressure on you to complete an action that you consider to be low priority, explain to them why you have set your priorities as you have. Selfishly guard your time. Avoid acting on low-priority activities when you have more important things on your to-do list. This can be difficult if the person who is putting you under pressure is more senior than you. You must still explain your priorities and let your superior know that they are jeopardizing your performance by insisting you carry out a low-priority task. It is preferable to be open and honest about conflicting pressures by regularly discussing priorities with your team.

USING TIME WISELY

The key to using time wisely is to have a good plan that recognizes not only what you have to do, but also how long it will take to carry it out. Set deadlines for the actions on your to-do list so that you allow enough time to complete them.

30 Refer to your to-do list to check you are meeting your deadlines.

31 Add contingency time to projects, so that you can cope with unforeseen delays.

ESTIMATING DURATION

Being in control means being able to complete the required actions on schedule. Work out what is involved in each activity and how long it will take. Put the high-priority ones first. Forecasting the duration of an action is vital, but it is often not easy – especially when the activity is new or reliant on others. Break actions down into stages and then estimate the time required for each task. Use historical data to help you. If someone has done a similar task before, ask them how long it took.

ACTING LOGICALLY

When you have estimated the time the actions on your to-do list will take, and have split them into manageable tasks, decide what to do first. Always bear in mind your top A-rated priorities and be careful to make an accurate estimate of the time it will take to carry them out. Now look at the relationship between the activities. For example, if you are organizing a training workshop, check the availability of the facilities before finding out when the participants are available.

Manager asks his colleagues to clarify several issues

WORKING SIMULTANEOUSLY ▶
See if there are any actions on your to-do list that could be resolved at a short meeting where questions can be addressed simultaneously and the job completed faster.

RELATING TASKS

Where a task is complex, take the time to draw a simple workflow diagram. Also called a network diagram, this reveals the order in which tasks must be completed. It also clarifies which tasks have the greatest time pressure. If there is a single task that has to be done before others can start, the network diagram will show you this and will allow you to trigger early action in this area. Look at the logic of the network diagram and see if it brings you some insight into how the tasks could be simplified and done faster.

▼ CONSIDERING ORDER
Analyze the tasks on your list; recognize some actions can only begin when others are complete; then schedule your tasks.

| Look at the critical tasks on your list | Decide on their natural order | Finalize the schedule for the project |

32 Make realistic estimates of how long tasks will take.

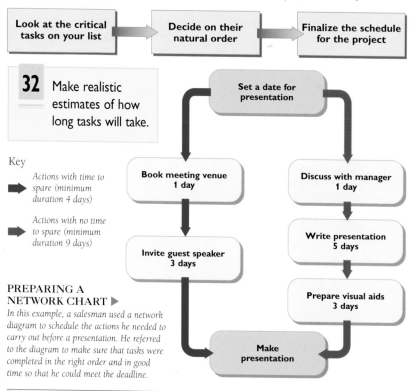

Key

→ *Actions with time to spare (minimum duration 4 days)*

→ *Actions with no time to spare (minimum duration 9 days)*

Set a date for presentation

Book meeting venue
1 day

Discuss with manager
1 day

Write presentation
5 days

Invite guest speaker
3 days

Prepare visual aids
3 days

Make presentation

PREPARING A NETWORK CHART ▶

In this example, a salesman used a network diagram to schedule the actions he needed to carry out before a presentation. He referred to the diagram to make sure that tasks were completed in the right order and in good time so that he could meet the deadline.

AVOIDING PROCRASTINATION

*P*rocrastination is the first obstacle to
overcome when you begin to tackle the
*tasks on your to-do list. Resolve never to
put anything off and always start activities
as early as possible. Be realistic about your
schedules and your workload.*

33 Get into the habit
of tackling difficult
issues first thing
in the morning.

34 Analyze the reason
why you are
postponing a task.

35 Remember that
procrastination
only makes
matters worse.

TACKLING HARD ISSUES

You may put a task off because you believe that
completing it is going to be difficult. However,
activities that cause you concern frequently turn
out to be easier than you expected if you act
immediately. For example, you may procrastinate
when you realize that a deadline is going to be
impossible to keep. Instead, contact the person
who is expecting you to finish the task on time
and tell them of the potential problem. Acting in
advance of missing a deadline may either get you
more time, or result in a suggestion as to how the
matter could be handled differently and in time.

DELIVERING
PROMISES

A reputation for delivering on
time will make your colleagues
regard you as dependable. It is
one of the best reputations to
have. Live by the slogan "under-
promise and over-deliver." Add
contingency time when you are
scheduling. Offer dates that you
are confident you can meet and,
if possible, deliver early.

*Manager
delegates
new project*

STARTING EARLY

Learn to start activities as early as you can. Even if the deadline is far enough in the future to make starting now unnecessary, it is good practice to "front-end load." This means doing as much as you can as early as possible. The opposite of front-end loading is leaving everything until the last minute. People who do that are much more likely to miss deadlines. They cut away all the time they might need to handle the unexpected. Suppose you are moving to a new office: if you leave packing until the day before the move, you make it impossible to do any other work that day. You have no contingency time to deal with unforseen problems or issues that might arise.

BEING REALISTIC ▶
Encourage your team to alert you to any problems that are likely to affect your deadlines, and then you will be able to take any necessary action.

THINGS TO DO

1. Look at your action list and decide which activities you could start on immediately.

2. Start on these tasks as soon as possible, even though the end date is some time in the future.

3. Make sure you plan contingency time in your new schedules.

Employee has too much work to do

Employee explains situation

Manager allocates extra help

Employee is overloaded and schedule is jeopardized

MAKING THINGS HAPPEN

People accept the leadership of colleagues who make a plan and keep control of it during its implementation. Be proactive and use your strengths to initiate action. Keep others informed of what you are doing and be flexible enough to adapt to the unexpected.

36 Gain a reputation for being decisive and acting with initiative.

▲ **BUILDING TEAMS**
At the start of a project, create a unified team. Hold a team meeting and turn it into a social occasion afterward to enable people to get to know each other.

LEADING WITH INITIATIVE

When you are approaching a new task or a series of tasks, work out what needs to be done and start decisively. When you are operating in a new area, it is easy to lack confidence and act hesitantly. Such hesitancy, however, passes itself on to others and leads to a loss of momentum. Think things through, then act decisively with leadership and authority. Work hard to get it right the first time. When a project begins, build up team spirit and make sure that everyone knows what their role in a new project will be.

POINTS TO REMEMBER

- Project objectives should be put in writing and circulated to all team members.
- All the team members should have a copy of current schedules.
- From time to time, get everyone together to monitor progress and share ideas and feedback.

TAKING LEADERSHIP ▶
It is essential that team members are aware of their roles. They will remain focused if they are kept informed.

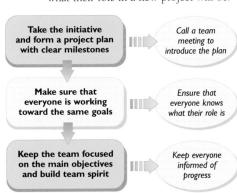

Take the initiative and form a project plan with clear milestones → *Call a team meeting to introduce the plan*

Make sure that everyone is working toward the same goals → *Ensure that everyone knows what their role is*

Keep the team focused on the main objectives and build team spirit → *Keep everyone informed of progress*

USING YOUR STRENGTHS

Remember that putting a wrong action right can take twice as long as getting it right the first time. Recognize your weaknesses and build on your strengths. Understand that in today's changing business environment more and more is expected of people. New tasks will feel uncomfortable and you will lack confidence – recognize and accept this as a natural human trait, but avoid letting it stop you from completing tasks. Maximize your chances of success, but also accept challenges.

> **39** Be involved in tasks that use your strengths.

▼ **ANALYZING YOURSELF**
Never let your weaknesses stop you from accepting new challenges. Learn to recognize your weaknesses and eliminate them or get around them if necessary. It is possible to counteract your weak points by planning ahead.

RECOGNIZING WEAKNESSES

Your technical knowledge is limited

You get nervous when people ask questions

You find it hard to do visuals spontaneously

WORKING WITH WEAKNESSES

Consult a technical expert for advice

Anticipate possible questions beforehand

Prepare visual aids before a presentation

> **37** Remain flexible so that you can adapt to new situations.

> **38** Change the plan if you anticipate a possible problem.

PLANNING FLEXIBILITY

No matter how well you have planned, some things will go wrong. There is a phrase in the military that states "no plan ever survives contact with the enemy." This rule applies equally in the business environment. Make sure you do not let your to-do list become set in stone. Review it regularly. Check whether or not the actions are still relevant, or if you need to change the list to reflect circumstances you were not expecting. Be open, admit problems when they occur, and remain flexible enough to respond to difficulties.

INVOLVING OTHERS

You may have to answer a call to action through the work of others as well as by your own endeavors. Make sure everyone involved in your to-do list understands their responsibilities, and aim to empower them to excel in their work.

40 Ensure that all team members are working toward the same goals.

41 Ask your team members to keep reviewing their actions with the customer in mind.

ALIGNING PEOPLE

If a team is to work together to improve overall performance, each member must agree on the group aim. A split in focus can cause conflict and adversely affect performance, particularly when team members come from different parts of the organization. Get them to understand and agree on the objectives of the team. Align the team toward the customer so that the team has the right focus and all members are focused on the same goal.

TEAM PLANNING

Your to-do list includes the priority you have set on each task, an estimate of how long it is going to take, and a schedule for when it is due to be completed. Ensure your team adopts the same planning method. Allocate responsibility for each specific task to one person. Make sure that people know the schedule and have agreed on dates – they should know when you expect them to finish a task. Each team member's to-do list must show who will do what and by when.

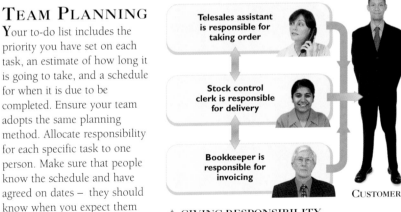

Telesales assistant is responsible for taking order

Stock control clerk is responsible for delivery

Bookkeeper is responsible for invoicing

CUSTOMER

▲ GIVING RESPONSIBILITY
In this example, the team members each have separate roles and responsibilities, but they are all working toward the same objective of getting the right product to the customer on time.

MOTIVATING TEAMS

ANALYZE
Take the time to look at the issues of a project yourself

QUESTION
Ask the team questions and gather relevant facts

LISTEN
Listen to your team members' points of view and opinions

RESOLVE
Work to resolve any conflicts or obstacles to action

INFLUENCE
Act as a leader to build consensus and motivate action

DO-IT-NOW LEADERSHIP

Leadership is the skill of persuading people to cooperate willingly to achieve a result. If you want people to join you in taking action now, you have to motivate them. Listen to them and understand what makes them enthusiastic about certain parts of their job. Your ability to have an impact through others is limited only by your ability to influence others to do it now. There are different leadership styles to motivate different people. Adopt the correct style, from dictatorial to consensus-based, to meet the needs of a situation.

DOS AND DON'TS

✔ Do ask questions to make sure the team is cooperating willingly.	✘ Don't assume that your team will agree with your plan.
✔ Do find out if there are any obstacles preventing an action from being carried out.	✘ Don't delegate and then relinquish all responsibility for the actions.
✔ Do check that no one is hiding resentment.	✘ Don't ignore the value of your team's ideas.

EMPOWERING PEOPLE

Most people want to do a good job. Delegate actions in such a way that the person to whom you are giving the task feels a sense of ownership. Encourage this by showing people that, once the task of delegation is complete, you have full confidence that they will achieve their objectives and complete the task on time and within budget. Understand that if you treat people as though they want to succeed and improve their performance, you will produce a strong environment of willing cooperation.

Manager expresses confidence

Employee takes ownership of task

▲ **DELEGATING TASKS**
Your staff will be motivated to achieve objectives on time and within budget if you show them you are confident in their ability to complete their tasks.

DECIDING LOGICALLY

If faced with several choices of initiatives, do-it-now people stop, think critically, and go through a decision-making process. Organize your thinking and improve your decisions.

VALUING THINKING

Good decision makers organize their thinking so that they can improve the speed and quality of the decisions they make. Spend time on analytical and creative thinking so that you can balance issues and make decisions that result in effective action.

42 Remember that good decisions are the result of effective thinking.

Perceptive

Resourceful

Practical

Original

Logical

▲ **QUALITIES OF A GOOD THINKER**
A do-it-now person is able to approach and think through issues effectively, in order to reach the best conclusions and make the most productive decisions.

THINKING CLEARLY

A logical decision-making process will enable you to become quicker at thinking things through and reaching "right-first-time" decisions. If you approach a decision in an organized manner and then meet the same situation again, the value of your original thinking is repaid. Well organized thinking will be of benefit to other people in your organization. Make sure others can make use of the thinking that you have put into a decision by taking notes about how you reached your conclusion.

43 Schedule time to think in your weekly planner.

44 Realize it is not a sign of weakness to admit you do not have an answer.

STARTING THE PROCESS

Take immediate and decisive action whenever possible, but do not act immediately if you are unclear how to choose the right option. Learn to think things through right to the conclusion of a project or activity before you set off on a course of action. Follow a consistent process that leads to a decision and a list of activities that will achieve your objectives quickly and efficiently. Do not put off making a decision, even a difficult one. Deal with it now and start the decision-making process. Even if you do not have the time to do all the thinking connected with a decision, remember the benefits to be gained from an early start.

FOCUSING CORRECTLY

Just as do-it-now people spend time and energy deciding what actions have a high impact on performance before they set priorities, they also make sure that they invest time thinking about and discussing the things that matter. There is no point in thinking of better ways of doing things if they do not have much impact on performance. Keep asking yourself, "So what?" to make sure you are on target.

45 Practice the decision-making process until it is automatic.

REMAINING ▶ FOCUSED
In this example, a manager found that he ran out of time to tackle the most important issues on his agenda during a meeting he had called. He realized how important it was to always keep his main objectives in mind.

CASE STUDY

A manager called a team meeting, intending to cover five agenda items. The last two items related to actions that would directly affect the team's performance. The team members all contributed toward the first few items on the agenda, which were about the layout of the new office accommodation. The manager spent time listening to every team member's view of the new layout. When the fourth item on the agenda was reached, a decision about entry to a new market, three team members had to leave for other appointments because the meeting had already overrun its time. The manager resolved to call another meeting to focus solely on the items which significantly impacted on the performance of the team. By keeping the main aims constantly in mind, the next meeting was more productive.

DEFINING FOCUS

Making a decision that will ensure the most effective outcome the first time relies on a good understanding of what is the best choice. Sometimes "best" means "within budget." In this case, you can only make a decision based on cost. In other instances, time is the crucial factor. Sometimes "best" means the best way to fix a problem or to exploit an opportunity. If your reputation is based on the quality and design of your product, you will need to spend the money and take the time necessary to get the best design.

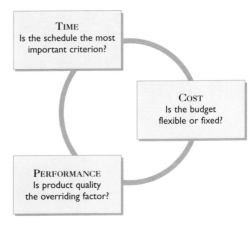

TIME
Is the schedule the most important criterion?

COST
Is the budget flexible or fixed?

PERFORMANCE
Is product quality the overriding factor?

▲ FOCUSING ON OUTCOMES
All projects have issues in terms of time, cost, and performance that must be balanced. There is little point in producing results on schedule if the budget is exceeded or quality is jeopardized.

46 Look for and focus on the most crucial outcome.

Sales manager points out importance of schedule

Business manager considers budget to be main priority

Customer service manager is concerned about quality

BALANCING ▶ PRIORITIES
In this example, the different department managers all have different priorities, but they must listen to each other's views in order to find the right balance between them.

THE EFFECTS OF EXTERNAL PRESSURES

PRESSURES	POSSIBLE IMPACT
The introduction of a new corporate computer operating system.	Current projects or tasks may be delayed while systems are put into place.
The implementation of new government regulations.	Procedures and projects may have to be adapted to fit new regulations, causing delays.
A change in the demands and expectations of a customer.	Customer demands may take a project over the expected budget and timescale.
Unexpected environmental elements, which disrupt schedules or damage products.	All resources may have to be diverted to deal with the unexpected issue.

CULTURAL DIFFERENCES

Many Japanese organizations adopt a technique called *nemawashi*. The term comes from horticulture, and means "to prepare the ground." *Nemawashi* aims to get every person who is involved in a project to support a strategy individually, long before the final decision is made. For example, this may involve inviting individuals to comment on recommendations. The process of resolving conflict and gaining consensus takes time, but means you are more likely to gain unanimous agreement on your decision from your colleagues.

ANTICIPATING PRESSURES

There are many external pressures that can affect your decisions, such as changes in software or the needs of a new customer. Many organizations are also affected by the pressure to create the quickest route a product or service takes to reach customers and to reduce the time each activity takes. Even if your job is to support those directly responsible for getting new products and services from inception to delivery, always recognize the effects of outside influences and make them influence your decision making. Take the time to check and think about every decision you make. Assess whether your decisions actually reduce the impact of external pressure.

 47 Remember that the perfect solution produced late is a free gift to the competition.

UNDERSTANDING CAUSES

Decision making is aimed at eliminating problems or removing barriers to opportunities. Understand the real causes of a problem in order to find solutions and make the best decision quickly, otherwise you may act but not solve the real issue.

48 Make sure you understand the real cause of recurring problems.

POINTS TO REMEMBER

- Team meetings should be arranged to identify problems and possible solutions.
- Temporary staff can be employed to cover for people on training.
- Your IT department should ensure office software is compatible and problem-free.

IDENTIFYING THE CAUSE

Before you can make the best decision on how to eliminate a problem, you need to be very clear about what the roots of the problem are. There are five possible areas where the roots of problems may lie: environment, manpower, machine, method, and material. When you are assessing a problem, ask yourself a series of questions to help you identify the area where the problem lies.

ASSESSING POSSIBLE PROBLEM AREAS

PROBLEM AREA	EXAMPLES
ENVIRONMENT Consider all aspects of working conditions.	Temperature; lack of space; difficulties in internal communication.
MANPOWER Assess your staff's level of skill and support.	Inadequate number of staff; poor skills; lack of training opportunities.
MACHINE Check the tools used for doing the job.	Poor state of repair; difficulty in getting spares; incompatible machinery.
METHOD Analyze how the business process works.	Inefficient department structures; tasks not done in the most effective order.
MATERIAL Examine supplies and suppliers.	Inadequate inventory checks; inappropriate materials; reliance on one supplier.

Pinpoint and examine the particular problem

Analyze all five possible areas where problems could arise

Even when you pinpoint a cause, keep checking for other causes

Once all possibilities have been analyzed, take action

FINDING MULTIPLE CAUSES

Analyze the problem until you have been through all five possible problem areas. If you find and act on the first cause, you may find that the problem persists because there is another root cause you had overlooked. If, for example, sales are down in a particular region and you find out that the sales people do not have all the appropriate brochures, provide them with the correct brochures, but keep checking for other possible causes. You may find that the region has less demand for the product.

◀ **COMPLETING THE ANALYSIS**
It is tempting when you have discovered a cause of a problem to take action to resolve it. However, keep analyzing all possibilities to make sure you have looked at all possible causes.

GETTING HELP

In any organization there is a huge amount of historical data about past performance. Consult this before making your decision. Do not disregard the opinions of your colleagues, who may have tackled a similar problem before. They may be able to give you a shortcut to finding a cause. Determine whether the problem is permanent or temporary. If it is a temporary issue and you make a decision to do nothing about it, will the problem simply disappear?

49 Consider asking customers for help in analyzing causes.

50 Avoid assuming the obvious cause is the only one.

Makes notes as colleague describes similar experience

◀ **TAKING ADVICE**
If you are trying to resolve an issue, you can get help from all kinds of people apart from your colleagues in the same organization. Ask your suppliers or your friends who may have met the issue before.

USING A PROCESS

There is a process for making decisions that has helped many do-it-now people get to the right choice quickly. Use this analytical decision-making process so that, with practice, you will be able to make good, effective decisions quickly.

51 Tell your team members and colleagues the process you use.

52 Discuss issues with others to help with your decision.

MAKING A DECISION ▼
There are three stages in the decision-making process: receive a trigger, consider all the issues involved, and then make a decision and carry it through.

PROCESSING DECISIONS

An analytical decision-making process has three parts. The input element is the stimulus to action and the facts or knowledge a person has to go on. The second element is the processing time, when the person uses a methodology to process their inputs. The third element, the output, is the quality and speed with which a decision is made. For better outputs, improve the information on which a decision is based, and the quality of the thinking.

Receive information	Think it through	Decide and act

UNDERSTANDING PURPOSE

The start of the decision-making process is understanding exactly what your decision aims to achieve. For example, if someone has left your team, the purpose of your decision is not simply to decide who to appoint to replace the person you have lost. Making that decision ignores the opportunity you have to evaluate and improve. Recognize that the purpose of your decision is how to get the person's work done. You may decide to appoint a replacement, but consider all the possibilities. Ask yourself if you could outsource the work or delegate it to another team.

53 Look at all the issues before you make a decision.

54 Analyze the purpose of the decisions you have to make.

LISTING YOUR CRITERIA

The quality of your decision depends on how well you understand the issues involved. Make a comprehensive list of these issues, or "decision criteria." If, for example, you are deciding between computer suppliers, your decision concerns not only their products, but also implementation, training, and support. Cost is also a criterion, although it is not always the best decision to buy the cheapest if there are other criteria on the list. Put criteria in order of importance by using a form of weighting such as 1 to 10 or "low," "medium," and "high."

POINTS TO REMEMBER

- Decision criteria should cover the issues thoroughly.
- Weighting can be used to pinpoint the key criteria that will have the most impact on the decision process.
- The ideal outcome should be identified even if you cannot be certain of meeting it.

55 Make a complete list of your decision criteria.

▼ PRIORITIZING CRITERIA

Most decisions are a trade-off between competing criteria. List the decision criteria involved and note what your ideal solution would be. When selecting a training seminar on decision making, for example, consider time, cost, and the flexibility of the approach.

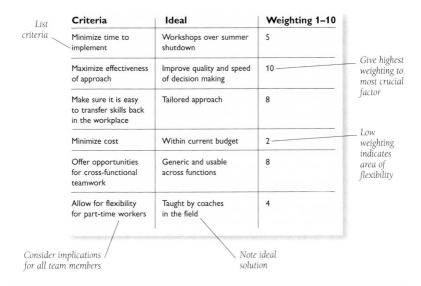

List criteria

Criteria	Ideal	Weighting 1–10
Minimize time to implement	Workshops over summer shutdown	5
Maximize effectiveness of approach	Improve quality and speed of decision making	10
Make sure it is easy to transfer skills back in the workplace	Tailored approach	8
Minimize cost	Within current budget	2
Offer opportunities for cross-functional teamwork	Generic and usable across functions	8
Allow for flexibility for part-time workers	Taught by coaches in the field	4

Give highest weighting to most crucial factor

Low weighting indicates area of flexibility

Consider implications for all team members

Note ideal solution

GENERATING OPTIONS

Consider first the option of continuing with the current solution. For example, suppose a painter has left the workshop. You could simply replace that person – a "manpower" solution. But look at your "materials" and see if there is an alternative that would enable you to buy components ready painted. Look at the other elements of cause and effect: "method," "machine," and "environment." Involve other people inside and outside your organization when you are looking for options.

Read trade journal for ideas on options

▲ **GATHERING DATA**
Gather as much information as possible. Browse trade magazines or the internet before you form a list of alternatives.

56 Aim to generate creative ideas with your team.

57 Make sure that new ideas are achievable.

CREATIVE THINKING

Rational thinking helps to ensure that you consider all logical options and make the "best" choice. However, if you do not look for creative alternatives at this stage in the process, you may find that your decision-making skills are not progressing. Creative thinking challenges the status quo. It helps you and your team to identify new ways of working that improve both quality and the time taken to get things done. Take the time to brainstorm with your team so that you can come up with new and innovative insights.

INSPIRING CREATIVE THOUGHT

The most effective individuals and teams combine rational and creative thinking. Help your team members improve their creative thinking skills. Ask probing questions that will provoke creative thought, different perspectives, and new ideas:

    If the current way of doing things becomes unusable, what would we do?

    How, if you were the team leader, would you start to make improvements?

    Could we begin to examine our objectives in a more productive or creative way?

    What do you think our competitors do in this area that we could aim to do better?

MAKING THE DECISION

Evaluate the options against each of the weighted criteria. At this stage, one or two of the options will be obviously less suitable. Drop the least suitable options. Remember you are looking for the best choice, not the first satisfactory one you find. Make a decision. Now think about how you "feel." If the decision "feels" wrong, check the criteria and weighting to make sure you have left nothing out.

POINTS TO REMEMBER

● You should make sure that the decision is being driven by the right issues.

● It is not always possible to get total consensus before the time has come to make a decision.

● Your team may need help to understand why you have to decide now.

Manager explains option

Weighs advantages and disadvantages

Points out a possible problem

DOS AND DON'TS

✔ Do read widely to find as many options as possible.

✔ Do look at the options others have discovered in similar circumstances.

✔ Do reject options if their disadvantages have become clear.

✘ Don't deal with too many options – create a short list.

✘ Don't assume that options that were viable in the past are still viable now.

✘ Don't keep an option open if most people have rejected it.

▲ CONSIDERING OPTIONS

In this example, a team discusses a new option put forward by a supplier. The manager encourages the whole team to discuss and weigh the options before making a final decision.

58 Plan when you will make a decision and do it then.

TAKING SHORTCUTS

When you have gone through the decision-making process a few times, it becomes your natural way of working. Learn how to short-circuit the thinking process when necessary, because some situations give you very little time to think.

59 Create an environment that encourages timely decision making.

60 Encourage your team to look for the best decision rather than take an easy option.

DECIDING NOW

You have to make a decision in time for it to be implemented – do not wait for perfect information if the delay will impact performance. Remember that the worst decision can often be to make no decision at all. When the time comes, make the decision and confidently inform those who need to know. In some organizations, a "blame" or "fear-of-failure" culture leads to employees making low-risk decisions rather than the best decisions.

DECIDING QUICKLY

If there is no time to adopt an analytical approach, use the VSAFE method of quick decision making. Look at the value each of the options gives you and consider how they would impact on your key performance measures. Then, consider how suitable the options are and how acceptable they are to those involved. It may be that some people will not welcome the decision. Be prepared to put off explaining it to them and try to get their agreement after the decision is made. Check that the option is feasible and long-lasting.

VALUE
Check option aids objectives

SUITABLE
Check option fits strategy

ACCEPTABLE
Check option is acceptable

FEASIBLE
Check option is achievable

ENDURING
Check option is long-term

USING THE VSAFE PROCESS ▶
Test your chosen option against the VSAFE model. If you do not get a positive answer to all of the criteria, look for another option or modify the chosen action plan. Encourage your team to adopt the same checking process.

CHOOSING A NEW SUPPLIER

CRITERIA	FACTORS TO CONSIDER
VALUE	Consider whether the option offers a significant reduction in operating costs.
SUITABLE	Analyze whether the option fits in with your overall business strategy of forming supplier partnerships.
ACCEPTABLE	Decide whether the supplier is already accepted and used in other parts of your organization.
FEASIBLE	Assess whether the supplier has the experience and capacity to deliver on time and within budget.
ENDURING	Consider whether any further change is required for the life of the product line.

61 Remember that if a decision is not an enduring solution it can lead to a recurrence of the issue.

EVALUATING RECOMMENDATIONS

Use other peoples' experience by welcoming recommendations. Check how they came to the decision by asking them what process they went through. If the process was thorough, your confidence in the recommendation will be higher than if no thought was given to it at all. Use the VSAFE generic questions to evaluate other peoples' suggestions. Think about a decision you have to make or a recommendation you have to decide on, and examine the options using the VSAFE technique right now.

USING INTUITION

Start to consider your thinking process. Intuitive thinking or "gut feeling" has a place in every successful person's toolbox. Intuition is the result of accumulated experience as well as skill, and the more experienced a person is, the more they can rely on their intuition – the subconscious mind. However, there are times when the thought process needs to take place in the conscious mind. In either case, if the answer is not clear, then stop and think.

TURNING A DECISION INTO ACTION

Once you have thought through and made a decision using a combination of the analytical process and creative thinking, put the decision into action now. Remember that until everyone involved has agreed to do their part, the decision is incomplete.

62 Remember, never take for granted another person's agreement to act.

63 Check how new commitments affect existing ones.

64 Make sure your decision will make an impact on your objectives.

COMMITTING TO ACT

Be aware that a decision to do something is different from a commitment to act. Put your action on your to-do list, give it the right priority, work out how long it will take, and allocate the time in your schedule for when you are going to do it. Check that the decision to act does not conflict with the other actions on your list. Does it mean that timings and priorities should change? Look at the to-do list as a whole, as well as a series of separate tasks. Finally, having checked the decision, make sure that, in its current form, it is going to address the underlying need.

IMPLEMENTING ▶ DECISIONS

In this example, a sales manager decided to send his assistant on a course. However, the training manager was unsure that the assistant was ready for the training. There was a risk that the decision would be left unimplemented.

CASE STUDY

A sales manager decided to send his sales assistant on a customer service course in order to improve his customer skills. To be approved for the course, the sales assistant had to explain to the training manager why he should be considered for the training. Places in the course were limited because of budget constraints, and the training manager was not convinced that the sales assistant merited a place in the course. The training manager explained to the sales manager that the sales assistant had not sounded convinced that the training course was right for him. The sales manager and his assistant then reviewed the decision together and agreed that it was still the right course of action. The assistant made a more confident presentation of his need for the training, and was offered a place in the next available course.

THINGS TO DO

1. Brief your team on the decision you have made.
2. Make sure everyone involved agrees with it.
3. Ask your team to prepare a plan of action.
4. Make sure the decision is carried through effectively.

GETTING OTHERS TO ACT

Communicate your decision to anyone who is involved and get their commitment to carry out their role. Often the right decision is rejected at the implementation stage because others do not fully understand the reasoning behind it. Improving the speed and quality of your thinking will have little impact if this happens. Spend time before and after making a decision to make sure the implementation goes smoothly. Speak to other people to make sure they understand the logical process involved in reaching your decision.

TAKING ACTION WITH CONFIDENCE

Your ability to get others to commit to an action is much stronger when you can support it with the reasoning of a logical process. But remember that enthusiasm and your own commitment and confidence will persuade others of the merits of your recommendations as much as logical or rational argument – one without the other is likely to result in rejection. Recognize that once someone has rejected a decision, it is much more difficult to persuade them to change their minds.

65 Take time to prepare your communications.

66 Combine rational arguments with enthusiasm.

CARRYING THROUGH A DECISION

When an appraisal meeting is held, a manager and an employee often agree on a number of actions to improve the employee's standard of work and their job skills. After an appraisal, however, when there are other demands on everyone's time, good intentions are often forgotten. Learn to be realistic when planning for an appraisal, and be persistent in ensuring that all targets are worked toward and met.

AGREEING ON ACTIONS ▶
A manager discusses and agrees a realistic action plan with the team member, and sets achievable dates for targets to be met.

Employee agrees on objectives and actions

GETTING ORGANIZED

Do-it-now people act once they have made a decision based on the information they need. Organize your information so that you can maximize your overall productivity.

GATHERING FACTS

Learn to use an analytical, systematic process for gathering facts. Develop a network of people and systems that gives you the facts you require at the time you require them, and make sure that information is always accessible.

67 Identify the information you need in order to make a decision.

68 Assess which contacts possess useful information.

69 Recognize the benefit of gathering the relevant facts before a meeting.

UNDERSTANDING YOUR NEEDS

The ability to make good decisions fast adds to the effectiveness of any team leader. Make sure that you recognize when you have insufficient knowledge to get to the right choice – no matter how hard and logically you think about it. Consider what the best sources of information are likely to be. When you know where you can get the information, you can estimate how much it will cost in money and in terms of your own time. Make sure that the advantage offered by the information is worth that time and cost.

USING YOUR NETWORK

When information is not available from your systems and archived files, it is often quickest and simplest just to ask your colleagues. It is an unfortunate fact that the best sources of information are often experts who are nearly always busy. Mail them or email them with a concise list of the information you need to make it as quick and easy as possible for them to give you the information – but accept that you may need to invest time in a face-to-face meeting to get the real facts you are looking for.

DIRECTOR

Ask your directors for historical data on projects

Ensure director passes down his business overview

Share views and information with your suppliers and external partners

MANAGER

Pass down relevant information to front-line staff

Solicit feedback and comments from frontline colleagues

BUILDING NETWORKS ▶
Take every opportunity to create good relationships with people who are able to provide information. Build a network of colleagues who can supply you with up-to-date and relevant information.

COLLEAGUES

70 Realize that the person who draws up the agenda tends to be in control of the meeting.

PREPARING FOR MEETINGS

If you are organized before a meeting, it will be more effective. If there is no agenda for a meeting, it can often result in a lack of focus and may not lead to the outcome you were seeking. When you schedule a meeting, send out an agenda beforehand so that people can bring the relevant information needed to address the meeting objectives. During the meeting, you will then be able to gather the facts you need in order to make quick decisions.

STRUCTURING YOUR INFORMATION

The point of storing data is to build up a source of information that increases your effectiveness. Make sure that the way you structure your files turns it into useful and accessible business knowledge that you can find quickly when you need to.

71 Review your filing structure to ensure it is appropriate.

72 Check that you have passed information to the person who is in a position to deal with it.

HANDLING DATA ONCE

File new information as soon as it arrives. Recognize that it takes time to put data into one place only to have to find it again and deal with it later. When you receive data, ask yourself, "If I put this information here, will my colleagues and I be able to find it immediately if required?" The answer should be, "Yes." Check that data is passed to the relevant individual. This can be a problem in many offices, whether they are big or small.

CLASSIFYING INFORMATION TYPES

Prepare to structure your files by first classifying the information that you will file together by "type." These types are the main categories that you deal with, such as project information or customer data. Categorize your filing system by these types and then break them into subcategories. For example, customer files will incorporate correspondence, such as proposals, and administration, such as order forms. This system applies to both paper-based or electronic filing.

Use folders to break down subcategories

Use plastic folders as subfiles within folders

▲ **STRUCTURING FILING**
Identify your main information types, and consider how you will break down hanging files into folders and subfiles so that information is easily accessible.

DEFINING YOUR INFORMATION STRUCTURE

Decide on the hierarchy of your folders and files. The most appropriate structure is the one that enables you to find information easily. Time spent structuring information is rarely wasted. List the hanging file (subcategory) headings within each information type. Decide what folders you need in each file. You may need subfiles within these folders. Check that your list has a logical hierarchy. Keep reviewing your filing system to make sure that it is up to date and efficient.

73 Keep your filing structure as simple as possible.

74 Encourage your team to adopt the same file structure.

CATEGORIZING YOUR FILING

INFORMATION TYPE	SUBCATEGORIES	FOLDERS
INTERNAL Information relating to personal performance.	● Personal files ● Performance records	● Job description; contracts ● Appraisals; objectives; training records
CUSTOMER FILES Data relating to your customers.	● Correspondence ● Administration information	● Proposals; reports; letters ● Order forms; contracts; letters of agreement
BUSINESS ENVIRONMENT Details regarding business changes and movements.	● Technical information ● Business magazines	● Product brochures and updates; market research ● Trade journals
PROJECT INFORMATION Information on your current projects.	● Project plans ● Supplier information	● Minutes of review meetings ● Product specifications and prices
TEAM PERSONNEL Information relating to staff and recruitment.	● Team member personal details ● Resumé information	● Objectives; appraisals; personal-development plans ● Resumé backfiles
ARCHIVES Backfiles on completed material and projects.	● Internal ● Customer	● One to two years' backfiles ● Three years' backfiles

NAMING YOUR FILES

Give your files and folders simple, generic names. For example, if you want to check the costs of your company car for the year, you will find a file called "Car costs" more quickly than a file with the name of the garage that services your car. For folders, use general labels such as "Invoices." Use a noun as the first word of a file or folder name. You will find a folder called "Prospects, current" more easily than one called "Current prospects." Aim to have a small number of large files rather than a large number of small files.

Store files in alphabetical order

Leave space within the drawer for ease of access

Align tabs so that you can see them all at a glance

Use color coding to categorize hanging files

TECHNICAL
PROJECTS
PERSONNEL
CUSTOMERS
ACCOUNTING

ARRANGING FILES ▲
Keep your files and folders in alphabetical order and arrange them so that their tabs are aligned, rather than staggered, so that you can remove a file without disrupting the filing system.

75 Make sure you can see the file label as soon as you open the filing cabinet.

ORGANIZING YOUR PHYSICAL FILES

In a hanging-file system, use colour to distinguish information types or the frequency of use. Clearly label the inserted folders and subfiles within the hanging files. The position of the label depends on how you see the hanging files as you open your desk or filing cabinet. You will not have to change hanging files very frequently, but you will have to move the insert folders as they become obsolete. You may also prefer to move a frequently used file to the front of the filing area.

76 Print out the list of your electronic filing for reference.

77 Make sure that all your information is easily available.

FILING ELECTRONICALLY

One of the benefits of storing files electronically is that the computer automatically produces your filing list. Match your email filing hierarchy to the one in your filing system. When you receive email, there are several ways to deal with it: act on it immediately and delete it; decide when you are going to deal with it and leave it in your inbox until complete; forward it to someone else for action and file it; or file it for future reading. Keep basic messages in your email filing system and transfer attached files into your master folder.

ARRANGING INFORMATION

Think about the frequency that you access types of files. Arrange your files so that you can access easily the ones you refer to most frequently. For regularly accessed electronic files, create a short-cut to them and keep them on your desktop. Analyze which files you need less often, such as technical information. Finally, when information is finished with, put it into an archive area.

78 Remember that you access some information daily.

▼ ACCESSING DATA
You will access some information, such as your address book, on a daily and weekly basis. Put manual files where they are easy to get to.

Electronic files are easily accessible

Contact numbers are at hand

Keep paperwork in your in-tray to a minimum

Small stationery items are kept in a divided drawer

Stick-on notes are kept by the phone

Files and folders are labeled for quick identification

UNDERSTANDING TECHNOLOGY OPTIONS

*A*s technology continues to leap
forward learn to make the most of
the electronic tools that can increase your
efficiency. Plan how you are going to use
technology to increase your effectiveness and
help you meet your performance objectives.

79 Take the time to design a logical electronic filing system.

80 Set aside time to learn new skills from training disks and computer tutorials.

NEW SOFTWARE ▼
*Take time to learn how to use
software that can help you
work more efficiently. Find
out how spreadsheets can
help you to organize data in
order to make quick and
effective decisions.*

ORGANIZING YOUR TOOLS

The personal computer has dramatically changed
the way we work. Think about how it can work
for you. Look at the tasks you use it for and analyze
the benefits of using a computer for tasks that you
normally do manually. Be critical – if using a
computer does not help in a situation, do not use
it. Some teams find it useful to have an office
dry-erase board to write down thoughts for their
colleagues' reference or input – a board can be a
useful part of a team's knowledge center. Put the
team's calendars on it or the team's to-do list.

*Training manager
explains main benefits
of new software*

*Employee puts
new skills into
practice*

COMPUTERIZING YOUR SCHEDULE

The most basic of tools is the to-do list. It lists what you are intending to do, the priority of each task, and the date for completion. Since it lies at the core of the do-it-now person's planning-and-control system, keep it as a shortcut on your desktop. It is also a good idea to keep an electronic calendar. This has the advantage of being able to display dates when, for example, the whole team will be available for a meeting. Be careful not to let it become a disadvantage by losing control of how you allocate your time. Remember to allow time for unexpected events. Consider blocking out parts of your schedule, even if you are not sure what you will be doing during that time, so that you can remain flexible.

81 Make your weekly planner accessible to your team.

82 Block out time in your schedule for unexpected issues.

▼ **ELECTRONIC PLANNER**
The electronic calendar is an excellent communications medium provided that it is kept up to date with changes to your to-do list and appointments.

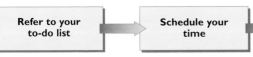

Refer to your to-do list ➤ **Schedule your time** ➤ **Update electronic schedule**

USING A PERSONAL DIGITAL ASSISTANT

When you are away from your desk, a Personal Digital Assistant (PDA) makes it possible to "take your office with you" and remain organized. It can contain a copy of your electronic calendar and has the ability to go online so that you can bring the master planner back at the office up to date. It also allows you to access the internet and your emails wherever you are. Use a PDA successfully by working out where you will keep your data and how using the PDA can make you more effective. Make sure the rest of your team knows your system.

▲ **KEEPING ORGANIZED**
If you spend a lot of time traveling, a laptop computer is a useful device. It allows you to keep your to-do list and other data with you all the time.

53

HARNESSING TECHNOLOGIES

S uccessful people stay on the leading
edge of technology. Understand that an
effective and stress-free business life depends
on keeping up with the opportunities offered
by available technologies so that you are
able to increase your proactivity.

83 Understand how new technologies can help maximize your performance.

USING TECHNOLOGY EFFECTIVELY

Become aware of the choices
your organization has made in
using technologies such as the
internet. You do not need to
understand how they work, just
what they can do for you. Access
the internet when you need to
gather information quickly. Find
out if your organization has an
intranet. This is a network that
uses the same technology as the
internet but is restricted to
one organization.

Sales manager researches competitors' products on internet

▲ **RESEARCHING ON THE INTERNET**
Information technologies have transformed the ways in which organizations can do business. Use the internet or intranet to access information from external and internal sources.

USING TECHNOLOGY WITHIN YOUR ORGANIZATION

TECHNOLOGY	USES WITHIN ORGANIZATION
EMAIL	Quick communication of messages; transference of electronic files
INTRANET	Access to organizational databases; shared corporate information
INTERNET	Online transactions; access to the World Wide Web
VIDEO CONFERENCING	Reduced travel budgets; improved global "team" communication

E-PROCUREMENT

Many suppliers offer an electronic procurement service. This is efficient because online product information can be kept up to date. When you order online, you normally receive an immediate email saying precisely what you have ordered. This identifies errors quickly, rather than waiting for written confirmation of the order or the delivery of the goods themselves.

USING SEARCH ENGINES

Search engines find information quickly, so that you can make efficient decisions and act. For example, if you have to buy computer supplies, use the internet to find the cheapest local supplier and place your order. Try different search engines to find the one that best suits your organization. Be careful not to waste time searching for data. View the internet as a vast library with an index system that can confuse users as well as assist them.

84 Take care to use your time on the internet efficiently when you are searching for data.

PUSHING AND PULLING

Become familiar with technologies that can work effectively for you. Use email to "push" information out to all the people on specified lists. Make sub-sets of lists for information that you need to send out and review them when requirements change. Use search engines to find information and "pull" the required data from the sources that they find. Set up an automatic search to inform you if new information has become available in the places you have asked it to look.

▼ USING TECHNOLOGY

In this example, a salesman receives an email. Before he replies, he "pulls" information he needs from the company intranet and decides which appropriate parties he needs to copy his email reply to.

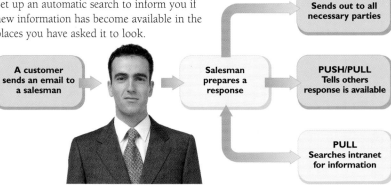

A customer sends an email to a salesman

Salesman prepares a response

PUSH Sends out to all necessary parties

PUSH/PULL Tells others response is available

PULL Searches intranet for information

HELPING OTHERS TO DO IT NOW

In the do-it-now culture, people pass on information for a purpose. Recognize that you are an important source of information for other people and that giving them information is not an end in itself, but part of the process of getting things done.

85 Make sure you send information only to the relevant people.

Look at the received information and decide on the necessary action to take

Consider whether to circulate this information to your team and colleagues

Think about whether it will help or hinder the other parties if they receive this information

Review the process to check you are sending data to the appropriate people

86 Ask people if they receive information that you send them from other parties.

CHOOSING WHAT TO SEND

The information you receive will enable you to think things through and take the necessary action. However, sometimes it is necessary to pass it on to others for their attention and action. Look at information critically as it arrives and get into the habit of asking, "Who else might benefit from this?" Make sure that you do not add to other people's "information overload" by unnecessarily circulating paperwork.

◀ ASSESSING RECIPIENTS
When deciding on a communication list, make sure that the information you are sending will have an impact on the receiver's ability to achieve their objectives.

DOS AND DON'TS

✔ Do keep information flow to minimum.	✘ Don't keep information flowing as a routine.
✔ Do check with people that they want information you are sending them.	✘ Don't assume that everyone needs the same level of detail that you do.
✔ Do communicate in the most effective style for each individual.	✘ Don't keep sending data to a person if they do not read it.

WORKING WITH PEOPLE'S PREFERRED STYLE

Take into account the individual when you are sending information rather than using one method for all. Remember that everyone has a preferred style of receiving information. Try to work to the other person's preference whenever possible to increase the probability that the information will be received and understood. Some people prefer you to speak to them. Others prefer to receive emails that they can read when it is convenient, rather than be interrupted by a conversation.

▲ COMMUNICATING WELL
Some people prefer information to be presented face-to-face rather than in writing. Adapt your method accordingly.

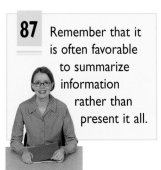

87 Remember that it is often favorable to summarize information rather than present it all.

PRESENTING KNOWLEDGE

Concentrate on the purpose of presenting knowledge rather than the knowledge itself. Do not necessarily pass on all the information you have. Think about what will happen afterward. If you are presenting information to senior people, for example, do not go into more detail than they need. A management summary may be all that is required to get them to accept your recommendations. Too much information or jargon can be counterproductive.

BEING OPEN TO QUESTIONS

People get a message when you present information at a meeting most effectively if they interact and ask questions. Cut the amount of information you present to a minimum, but make sure that people realize that you are expecting them to ask questions:

❝ I am available to answer any questions you may have on this subject. ❞

❝ I have reduced these facts to the bare bones; if you need more details, please ask. ❞

❝ Please feel free to ask questions at any time during the presentation, or at the end. ❞

❝ If some people want further details, I am available for questions after the meeting. ❞

Learning from Experience

One way to become more organized is to capture all the lessons you have learned from past experience. Think about how to make the best use of your experience.

Focusing on Improving

The pressures of modern business life mean that you can never relax and think that you are working as effectively as possible. Always be on the lookout for ways to improve. Remember, you have to change as fast as the business world is changing.

88 Realize that, if you stop learning, you will soon stop being effective.

Questions to Ask Yourself

Q Do I regularly ask customers if they are satisfied?

Q How could we adapt the service we offer?

Q Do I continually review processes to see how to change them for the better?

Q Do I keep up-to-date with changes in business?

Q Do I listen to other people's views?

Adapting to Change

Recognize that the business climate in which your organization operates changes continuously. Your customers expect more from you, and competitors frequently improve their performance and try to prove that they offer a better service than you. It is no longer satisfactory to show up to work to do the same job that you did yesterday – you must continuously improve what you do and the way that you do it. For example, seek regular feedback from your customers to keep abreast of their requirements and to assess their levels of satisfaction with your performance.

PLAN Get into the habit of planning actions thoroughly	Work out how you are going to achieve an objective
EXECUTE Carry out the plan and adapt it where necessary	Make sure you keep your focus on your objective
REFLECT Think about how you could improve processes	Assess the implications of all your actions
LEARN Make sure you learn lessons from your past actions	Look at procedures you could change

▲ USING THE PERL CYCLE
If you adopt the PERL-cycle principle, you will become more and more effective, and you will be equipped to avoid the repetition of mistakes and the recurrence of problems.

USING THE PERL CYCLE

The four stages of the PERL cycle – plan, execute, reflect, and learn – allow you to make the most of and learn from experience. Once you have planned and executed some of the activities on your to-do list, reflect on how well you have achieved your aims and what you could have improved. Suppose you have just completed the installation of equipment. Was the customer happy? What could you have done better? Always aim to plan time into your schedule to reflect.

89 Put time aside to reflect on ways to improve processes.

KEEPING A WINNING METHOD

If you and the team have achieved a good result, put yourself in the best position to repeat the process. The PERL process gives the do-it-now person the opportunity to reapply the things that worked and eliminate those that did not. The time you spend on reflecting at the end of a successful activity will be repaid the next time you do something similar. Keep the successful project plans for future reference.

▲ REVIEWING A PROJECT
Meet with your customer at the end of a project to review how it went and to analyze procedures to see if there are any you would change next time.

CAPTURING BEST PRACTICES

In addition to learning from experience, it is possible for whole teams or organizations to learn from each other. Experiences can be documented and distributed – often called "capturing best practices" – as templates for future projects.

90 Build on past experiences and benefit from improved decisions.

91 Encourage your team to work with templates.

92 Record successful decisions as templates.

USING TEMPLATES

You can formalize the process of reflecting and learning by documenting successful methods in the form of templates. A template provides standard ways of doing things and lists methods that have worked in the past. For example, all organizations select suppliers of goods and services from time to time. Some members of the team may prioritize quality, while others consider after-sales service to be of paramount importance. All factors common to purchasing decisions could be captured in the creation of a "supplier selection template."

Notes down actions that worked well

▼ **ANALYZING PROCESSES**
In this example, a production team meets to discuss their standard processes, so that they can form a template.

Production manager describes how he handled a past project

INSTITUTING ROUTINES

Once you have identified best-practice approaches, make sure you and your team follow them. They are useful in many instances, from preparing course material to building a system of fault recording. You will find that, once you have followed the routine a number of times, you will no longer have to consciously think about how you are working. You will have internalized the template and will be automatically following best practice. To get consistency, encourage the use of these routines throughout the team.

THINGS TO DO

1. Look at how you could improve your routines.

2. Use a consistent approach to templates so that your team gets used to them.

3. Build a library of completed templates that you can learn from.

USING TECHNOLOGY

Capturing and sharing best practices can be streamlined. Put the template on a spreadsheet and use examples so that others can easily follow. Make it available in a file that everyone can access or send it out by email. For example, suppose you have recently recruited two new people. One has worked out well and the other finds the job difficult. You can capture the differences between the two and build a template that lists the attributes future candidates will have to demonstrate.

93 Make sure that your team can access templates on a file server quickly and easily.

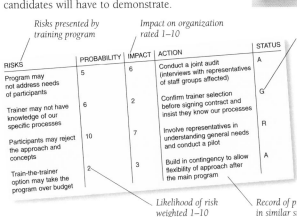

Risks presented by training program

Impact on organization rated 1–10

Issues rated as "red," "amber," "green"

RISKS	PROBABILITY	IMPACT	ACTION	STATUS
Program may not address needs of participants	5	6	Conduct a joint audit (interviews with representatives of staff groups affected)	A
Trainer may not have knowledge of our specific processes	6	2	Confirm trainer selection before signing contract and insist they know our processes	G
Participants may reject the approach and concepts	10	7	Involve representatives in understanding general needs and conduct a pilot	R
Train-the-trainer option may take the program over budget	2	3	Build in contingency to allow flexibility of approach after the main program	A

◀ **USING TEMPLATES**
This template reflects the risk analysis that was followed for gauging how likely a training course was to achieve its objectives. Knowledge was then shared across the organization.

Likelihood of risk weighted 1–10

Record of previous action in similar situations

SHARING INSIGHTS

When people are achieving results, they sometimes have completely new ideas that can improve their performance and productivity. These can be real breakthrough ideas. Make sure that you take advantage of new ideas and insights.

94 Share winning insights with your team and business partners.

POINTS TO REMEMBER

- Your ideas and insights may be of value to your colleagues.
- Information technologies have made it possible for insights to be shared globally.
- Technology allows the sharing of insights in "real-time" and can be acted on immediately.

95 Thank people for insights so that they share more.

FILING INSIGHTS

As people complete tasks, they often find that they have gained information that may be of value to others. This information is called an "insight." It is different from a template in that it comes from an understanding that a task can be done better. For example, a salesman in New York loses an order because he pitched the wrong Unique Selling Proposition (USP) against a particular competitor. He now has an insight into how to sell against that competitor. If he logs this in an electronic "insights file" the next day, his colleague in Chicago can check the file and adapt his proposition to win an order.

CASE STUDY

Bill was the project leader of a mobile-telephone production line in the US. His manager noticed that the European manufacturers of the same product had a significantly lower production cost. He asked Bill to get in touch with the relevant project leader. Bill discussed the matter on the telephone with Olga, the person responsible in Germany, and discovered that she had found a source of materials in Asia that was much cheaper than the supplier Bill was currently using. Bill switched suppliers and his costs came down to match those in Germany. Bill and Olga agreed to set up a shared file on the organization's intranet recording the changes that they made to their production methods. This meant that both sites could share insights and they both improved their performance over time.

◀ **LEARNING FROM OTHERS**
The systematic sharing of new ideas and insights helps to spread best practice around an entire organization, even on a global basis. The benefits are outlined here by the interaction between a project leader in the US and his European counterpart in Germany.

CLOSING THE LOOP

In a time of increasing staff turnover and mobility, it is vital that insights are formally captured in an accessible file and shared. For example, use your team's accumulated knowledge to maintain customer satisfaction or stay ahead of the competition. Take time to write down and share insights with others. Give people access to insights by allocating key words that will make it easy for others to find information.

Sales assistant is having difficulties with a customer

Sales manager relates past experience of dealing with customer

Notes insights for future reference

**COMMUNICATING ▶
EXPERIENCES**
By talking to your colleagues about your experiences, you can significantly impact the overall performance of the team.

96 Make sure your team members record and file information.

INVOLVING THE TEAM ▼
Sharing insights with your team means that all team members have access to information and are therefore in a better position to make quicker decisions and act immediately and efficiently.

PASSING INSIGHTS ON

Aim to present insights to the team in an interesting way. An old but effective method of sharing information is to present it in the form of a story that everyone can understand and relate to. This approach is useful for coaching and mentoring. Avoid just telling the member of staff what the rule is, give them a real example. For example, a manual on setting up exhibition stands will include a precise specification for the handrails. This is less likely to communicate what needs to be done than telling the story of an accident caused by ineffective handrails.

Team shares insights	▶	Information is accessible	▶	Decisions can be made quickly

LEADING A BALANCED LIFE

All work and no play is a recipe for becoming less productive at work and less fulfilled at play. If you are to continue to build on and develop your efficiency at work, it is important to maintain a healthy balance between work and leisure.

97 Remember that discussing matters with others reduces stress.

98 Use a separate room for work at home if possible.

99 Schedule time in your week for regular exercise.

WORKING FROM HOME

As an effective member of a team, you develop good methods for taking action, thinking things through, and gathering information. It is equally important to be an effective member of a family or a circle of friends. Avoid being a "workaholic." Take time to reflect on the balance in your life – how much time do you spend at work and how much at play? There are ways of adjusting this: you may be able to work from home one or two days a week; or perhaps your workload has increased so much that you can justify another team member.

| Assess your workload | ▶ | Talk to your senior manager | ▶ | Delegate responsibility |

KEEPING FIT

Some people put things off because they are not feeling completely healthy. There is increasing evidence that people who are physically fit cope with the challenges of modern business life better than those whose work schedules leave them little time for exercise. This does not mean that you have to run marathons, but that you should get some exercise at least twice a week. Try to put aside a regular time for this so that people know when you are not available.

▲ DISCUSSING OPTIONS
If your workload is too heavy, talk to your senior manager. The problem could be solved by delegating tasks and agreeing to give up responsibility for certain tasks.

100 Remember that exercise increases your energy levels.

▲ **MAKING TIME TO RELAX**
Develop one of the most important abilities any working person needs – the ability to go out of the workplace door and leave business stress and worry where they belong.

101 Realize that overwork and stress can impair your ability to make effective decisions.

MANAGING STRESS

Your efficiency will increase rather than go down if you take regular breaks from intense activity. People who maintain their effectiveness develop the ability to take fifteen minutes in the middle of the day to unwind and prepare themselves for the challenges of the afternoon. Aim to really get away from it – do not spend this time with your colleagues. Of course, there are times in even the best-regulated lives when long periods of hard work are required. If this is happening to you on a regular basis, however, reevaluate your working processes to find and deal with the underlying causes.

HEALTHY EATING

Always have a nutritious breakfast so that you are able to start the day feeling full of energy and ready to face the most difficult tasks on your to-do list first. During the day, make sure you take breaks to recharge your batteries, and then you will be able to work at your optimum efficiency. If you are in the habit of snacking, take fruit to work with you, because it is rich in vitamins and fiber. Quick fixes of sugar-rich chocolate can boost your energy momentarily, but leave you feeling tired and prone to procrastination later, which

can have an effect on your effeciency. Get into the habit of drinking plenty of refreshing water during the day and avoid stimulants such as tea or coffee, which can heighten stress.

EATING WELL ▶
A healthy, balanced diet will give you the energy to face the challenges of modern life.

ASSESSING YOUR SKILLS AS A DO-IT-NOW PERSON

Evaluate your ability to act effectively and on time by responding to the following statements, marking the option closest to your experience. Be as honest as you can: if your answer is "Never", circle option 1; if it is "Always," circle option 4, and so on. Add your scores together, and refer to the Analysis to see how well you scored. Use your answers to identify the areas that most need improvement.

OPTIONS
1 Never
2 Occasionally
3 Frequently
4 Always

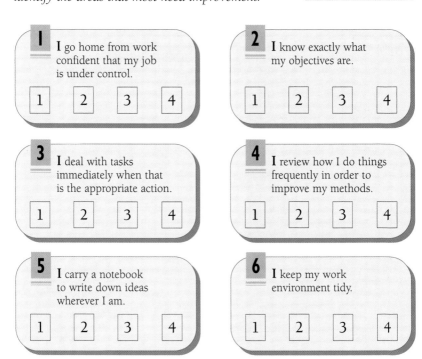

1 I go home from work confident that my job is under control.

1   2   3   4

2 I know exactly what my objectives are.

1   2   3   4

3 I deal with tasks immediately when that is the appropriate action.

1   2   3   4

4 I review how I do things frequently in order to improve my methods.

1   2   3   4

5 I carry a notebook to write down ideas wherever I am.

1   2   3   4

6 I keep my work environment tidy.

1   2   3   4

7 I respond to all incoming communications immediately.

| 1 | 2 | 3 | 4 |

8 I tell people if I have decided not to take action on something.

| 1 | 2 | 3 | 4 |

9 I allocate an up-to-date status to all the actions on my to-do list.

| 1 | 2 | 3 | 4 |

10 I deal with matters that are important before they become urgent.

| 1 | 2 | 3 | 4 |

11 I know what actions need to be done first.

| 1 | 2 | 3 | 4 |

12 I under-promise and over-deliver.

| 1 | 2 | 3 | 4 |

13 I make plans that take account of my weaknesses.

| 1 | 2 | 3 | 4 |

14 I use appropriate styles of leadership.

| 1 | 2 | 3 | 4 |

15 I make decisions at the right time.

| 1 | 2 | 3 | 4 |

16 I obtain other people's agreement with my decisions on an individual basis.

| 1 | 2 | 3 | 4 |

17 I look for all the causes of problems.

1 2 3 4

18 I list my decision-making criteria before I make a decision.

1 2 3 4

19 I think creatively as well as rationally.

1 2 3 4

20 I make use of a checking procedure to make sure I have made the right decision.

1 2 3 4

21 I follow up decisions by adding the actions to my to-do list.

1 2 3 4

22 I take time to prepare before I communicate with other people.

1 2 3 4

23 I find the information I need on a regular basis.

1 2 3 4

24 I keep the structure of my filing system up to date.

1 2 3 4

25 I file things as I go along.

1 2 3 4

26 I use technology when it is appropriate.

1 2 3 4

27 I find the information I need by searching sites on the internet.

| 1 | 2 | 3 | 4 |

28 I try to think about communication from the other person's point of view.

| 1 | 2 | 3 | 4 |

29 I make sure that I learn from my mistakes.

| 1 | 2 | 3 | 4 |

30 I document my routines and actions so I can make use of them in the future.

| 1 | 2 | 3 | 4 |

31 I share useful experiences with my colleagues.

| 1 | 2 | 3 | 4 |

32 I keep a good balance between work and leisure.

| 1 | 2 | 3 | 4 |

ANALYSIS

Now that you have completed the self-assessment, add up your total score and check your performance by reading the corresponding evaluation. Whichever level of skill you have reached in doing it now, it is important to remember that there is always room for improvement. Identify your weakest areas, and refer to the relevant section and chapters for practical advice and tips to help you develop and refine your skills.

32–64: There are areas you need to improve to be a do-it-now person. Implement some of the suggestions in the book now.

65–95: You are good at getting things done on time, but certain areas need improvement.

96–128: You are reliable and effective, but do not become complacent. Keep striving to improve your performance.

INDEX

A

ABC analysis, 22
actions:
  appraisal meetings, 45
  committing to act, 44
  effective action, 12–13
  stimulating action, 10–11
  to-do lists, 20–23, 24
address books, 51
agendas, meetings, 47
analysis:
  ABC analysis, 22
  analysis paralysis, 17
  causes of problems, 36–37
  decision-making processes,
  38–41
  of processes, 12
  self-analysis, 29
anticipation, decision making, 35
appraisal meetings, 45
archives, 49, 51

B

balanced life, 64–65
best practices, capturing, 60–61
"blame" culture, 42
brainstorming, 40

C

calendars, 16
  electronic calendars, 53
capturing best practices, 60–61
categories, filing systems, 49
causes of problems, 36–37
change, adapting to, 58
color, filing systems, 50
communication:
  deciding not to act, 19
  emails, 16
  passing on information, 56–57
  responding to, 14–15
  sharing insights, 62–63
computers, 52–53
  electronic diaries, 53
  electronic filing systems, 51
  laptop computers, 53
conflicts, building teams, 30
contingency time, 26, 27
costs, decision-making criteria,
  34, 39
creative thinking, 40
criteria, decision making, 39, 41
cultural differences, 35

D

data:
  dealing with, 16
  decision-making processes, 40
  definition, 17
  presentation, 16
  structuring, 48–51
  waiting for, 17
deadlines:
  avoiding procrastination, 26
  "front-end loading", 27
decision making:
  gathering facts, 46–47
  logical decisions, 32–45
  options, 11
  processes, 38–41
  shortcuts, 42–43
  taking action, 44–45
  understanding causes of
  problems, 36–37
  VSAFE method, 42–43
delegation, 15, 31
delivery dates, dependability, 26
dependability, 26
desks, organizing, 51
diagrams, workflow, 25
diet, 65

E

emails, 54
  dealing with, 51
  gathering facts, 47
  passing on information, 57
  Personal Digital Assistant
  (PDA), 53
  presentation of, 16
  "pushing" information with, 55
effective action, 12–13
electronic calendars, 53
electronic filing systems, 51
electronic procurement services,
  55
empowering people, 31
environment, causes of problems,
  36

exercise, 64
experience, learning from, 58–65
external pressures, 35

F

facts see data; information
"fear-of-failure" culture, 42
feedback:
  building teams, 28
  improving performance, 58
filing systems:
  dealing with data, 16
  electronic, 51
  naming files, 50
  structuring information, 48–51
fire-fighting, 13, 23
flexibility, 29
focus, decision making, 34
folders:
  hanging-file systems, 50
  naming, 50
  structuring information, 49
forecasting, time management, 24
"front-end loading", time
  management, 27

H

hanging files, 49, 50
home, working at, 64

I

ideas, recording, 14
in-trays, 16, 51
information:
  dealing with, 16
  decision-making processes, 11,
  40
  definition, 17
  gathering facts, 46–47
  passing on, 56–57
  presentation of, 16, 57
  "pushing" and "pulling", 55
  search engines, 55
  sharing insights, 62–63
  structuring, 48–51
  waiting for, 17
insights, sharing, 62–63
internet, 53, 54
  electronic procurement, 55
  research on, 54

search engines, 55
intranets, 54, 55
intuition, 43

J
Japan, cultural differences, 35
job descriptions, 8

L
laptop computers, 53
leadership:
    motivation, 31
    proactive, 28
learning, capturing best practices, 60–61
lifestyle, 64–65
lists see to-do lists
logical decisions, 32–45

M
machinery, causes of problems, 36
manpower, causes of problems, 36
materials, causes of problems, 36
meetings:
    appraisal meetings, 45
    preparing for, 47
methods, causes of problems, 36
motivation, leadership, 31

N
naming files, 50
nemawashi technique, 35
network diagrams, 25
networks, gathering facts, 47

O
objectives, 8–9, 28
options, decision making, 40–41
outcomes, decision making, 34

P
paperwork, dealing with, 16, 51
    see also data; information
perfectionism, 17
performance, decision making, 34
PERL cycle, 59
Personal Digital Assistant, 53
personal organizers, 14
physical fitness, 64
presentation, of data, 16, 57
pressures, decision making, 35
priorities:
    ABC analysis, 22
    criteria, 39

decision making, 34
time management, 23
workflow diagrams, 25
proactive people, 6, 7
    becoming proactive, 13
    deciding not to act, 18–19
    leadership, 28
    proactive thinking, 20
problems:
    contingency time, 26, 27
    deciding not to act, 18–19
    understanding causes of, 36–37
processes:
    analyzing, 12
    decision making, 38–41
    improving, 12
procrastination, avoiding, 26–27
procurement, electronic, 55
projects, reviewing, 59
purpose, decision making, 38
put-it-off people, 7

R
rational thinking, 40
recommendations, evaluating, 43
recording ideas, 14
relaxation, 65
research, on internet, 54
reviewing projects, 59
risk analysis, 61
roles:
    building teams, 28
    knowing objectives, 8
    team planning, 30
routines:
    analyzing processes, 12–13
    capturing best practices, 61

S
schedules:
    ABC analysis, 22
    building teams, 28
    team planning, 30
search engines, internet, 55
short-cuts, decision making, 42–43
"so what?" response, 18–19, 33
software, 52
spreadsheets, capturing best practices, 61
status, to-do lists, 21
strengths, proactive leadership, 29
stress, 6, 65
structuring information, 48–51
subconscious mind, intuition, 43

T
teams:
    aligning people, 30
    brainstorming, 40
    building, 28
    consensus, 41
    decision making, 41
    motivation, 31
    sharing insights, 62–63
technology, 52–55, 61
templates, capturing best practices, 60–61
thinking:
    creative thinking, 40
    rational thinking, 40
    valuing, 32–35
time, decision making, 34
time management, 24–25
    avoiding procrastination, 26–27
    being selfish with time, 23
    contingency time, 26, 27
    electronic calendars, 53
    estimating duration, 24
    "front-end loading", 27
    to-do lists, 20–23, 24
    workflow diagrams, 25
to-do lists, 20–23, 53
    ABC analysis, 22
    allocating status, 21
    committing to act, 44
    estimating duration of tasks, 24
    PERL cycle, 59
    reviewing, 29
    taking and keeping control, 23
    team planning, 21, 30
    "write on, wipe off" boards, 52
triggers, stimulating action, 10–11

U
Unique Selling Proposition (USP), 62
urgent actions, 23

V
valuing thinking, 32–35
video conferencing, 54
VSAFE method, decision making, 42–43

W
weaknesses, recognizing, 29
weighting criteria, 39, 41
workflow diagrams, 25
"write on, wipe off" boards, 52

ACKNOWLEDGMENTS

AUTHORS' ACKNOWLEDGMENTS

The authors were very impressed by the team of highly skilled people involved in producing this book. Adèle Hayward at DK added greatly to the content of the book before it went to the designers. Also at DK, we would like to thank Nigel Duffield and Jamie Hanson for their help in the overall design and structure. Laura Watson added hugely to the project with her ideas on presentation, while Kate Hayward and Jane Baldock are encouraging motivators as well as meticulous editors. Our thanks to all of them.

PUBLISHER'S ACKNOWLEDGMENTS

Dorling Kindersley would like to thank the following for their help and participation:

Editorial Mark Wallace
Indexer Hilary Bird; **Proofreader** Polly Boyd; **Photography** Gary Ombler.

Models Roger André, Philip Argent, Clare Borg, Marian Broderick, Angela Cameron, Anne Chapman, Kuo Kang Chen, Brent Clarke, Russell Cosh, Roberto Costa, Patrick Dobbs, Vosjava Fahkro, Emma Harris, Kate Hayward, Richard Hill, Cornell John, Lucy Kelly, Janey Madlani, Sotris Melioumis, Roger Mundy, Karen Murray, Chantal Newall, Mutsumi Niwa, Kiran Shah, Lynne Staff, Suki Tan, Peter Taylor, Anastasia Vengeroua, Ann Winterborn, Roberta Woodhouse, Wendy Yun; **Makeup** Nicky Clarke

Picture researcher Laura Roberts; **Picture librarian** Melanie Simmonds

PICTURE CREDITS

The publisher would like to thank the following for their kind permission to reproduce their photographs:

Key: a=above; b=bottom; c=center; l=left; r=right; t=top
Corbis: R W Jones 28cl; Peter Turnley 53br; Premium Stock 59br;
Powerstock Photolibrary / Zefa: 65tl
The Stock Market: 4–5; 19bl;
gettyone.stone: Walter Hodges 6bl

AUTHOR'S BIOGRAPHY

Andy Bruce is the founder of the internet-based management software company, SofTools.net. Following the completion of his MBA, he has spent the last nine years developing practical business tools to help improve the performance of individuals and teams.

Ken Langdon has a background in sales and marketing in the computing industry. As an independent consultant, he has taught management techniques and strategy courses in the US, Western Europe, and Australasia, and he is the author of a number of books including *Key Accounts are Different* and *Smart Things to Know About Business Finance*.